EDITOR: LEE JOHNSON

MEN-AT-ARMS SE

THE GRENADIER GUARDS

Text by

GENERAL SIR DAVID FRASER

Additional research by

R. J. MARRION & D. FOSTEN

Colour plates by

ANGUS McBRIDE

First published in Great Britain in 1978 by
Osprey, an imprint of Reed Consumer Books Ltd.
Michelin House, 81 Fulham Road,
London SW3 6RB
and Auckland, Melbourne, Singapore and Toronto

Reprinted 1996

ISBN 0 85045 284 8

Filmset in Great Britain
Printed through World Print Ltd., Hong Kong

Foreword

by H.R.H. The Duke of Edinburgh

The existence of a Regiment, just as the state of the world, is due to actions and decisions of long ago. The story of the Regiment now known as the First or Grenadier Regiment of Foot Guards started in Bruges in 1656, and everything about the Regiment today, its title, organization, uniform, equipment, battle honours, traditions and duties derive from events – dramatic, tragic and triumphant – of 300 years of history.

Whatever the changes in circumstances during this long period, as this booklet makes abundantly clear, the Grenadiers have given a shining example to friend and foe alike of the true mettle and fighting qualities of the British soldier in triumph and adversity.

Philip

Introduction

Originally a grenadier was a soldier who threw a grenade. The grenadier formed part of most European armies from the late 17th Century onwards. Grenadier companies existed in all British Infantry battalions. Later grenadiers in Infantry battalions were the senior, right flank companies, composed of the tallest men.

In the United Kingdom, for the last 150 years, 'The Grenadiers' have meant one thing only – the Regiment entitled The Grenadier Guards, or to give them their full title 'The First or Grenadier Regiment of Foot Guards', the Senior Regiment of Foot in the British Army and the only Regiment to have won its official title of 'Grenadiers' in battle. This book is the story of the Grenadier Guards, their beginnings, some of their battles, their customs and traditions from their formation as 'The Royal Regiment of Guards' in 1656 down to our own times.

What is, and what was a Regiment? A Regiment was a body of fighting men, organised originally into a number of companies each commanded by a Captain, each with its own Colour or Standard, a huge flag, a great deal larger than the present Colours carried on ceremonial occasions. The Company Colour could be seen and recognised above the heads of fighting men, showing where their rallying point and centre was. A Regiment was recruited, officered, and in early years to a large extent, financed by a Colonel who had a commission from the Sovereign so to do. The Colonel, who often gave his name to the Regiment, had to be a man of considerable wealth and was likely to have great power and influence with wide responsibilities in the Army, so he would entrust the detailed management of the Regiment to a Lieutenant-Colonel, his deputy and executive.

It followed that the position of the Colonel was of great significance. He was the Father of his Regiment and, to a large extent, its proprietor. In the disturbed days of the 17th and 18th centuries the Sovereign depended absolutely on the loyalty of the Guards Regiments and thus on the complete trustworthiness of the colonels. In consequence colonels were likely to change with changes in political climate.

In such a period the Sovereign needed to have around him certain picked troops as Guards on whose devotion he could rely, whose Colonel would be a man of distinction and proven loyalty, and whose privilege it would be, not only to take the right of the line – the position of honour – in battle, but to undertake the personal protection of the Sovereign and the Royal Family. Thus there were formed, as in all the monarchies of Europe, troops known as 'Household Troops', 'Royal Guards' or in Great Britain simply 'The Regiments of Guards'.

As the 18th Century, with its ceaseless wars against France, wore on and as the British Regular Army developed, companies of Regiments became permanently grouped in Battalions, each with its own Commander. The arrangement led to the end of the system whereby each Company, semi-

'Blenheim: crossing the Danube', from the watercolour by Richard Simkin.

'After the Battle', from an oil painting by P. H. Calderon in The Regimental Collection.

independent, had centred around its own Colour. By the middle of the 18th Century we find each battalion ordered to carry only two colours which became 'The Battalion Colours', one always known as the King's (or Queen's) Colour, which in Regiments of the Line was the Union Flag representing allegiance to the State, but in the Household Regiments was a crimson flag with a Royal Emblem representing personal association with the Sovereign; and the other, known as 'The Regimental Colour', which in Regiments of the Foot Guards was one of the old Company Colours taken in turn as a new one was required.

A Regiment consisted of varying numbers of battalions just as originally it had consisted of varying numbers of companies. In the First or Grenadier Regiment of Foot Guards there were, from the time that battalions were permanently formed, three battalions, although in the late 17th Century there had for a time been four. These were increased by a fourth battalion in the War of 1914–18; again increased by three, the 4th, 5th and 6th Battalions, in the War of 1939–45. In 1961, as part of a reduction of the Regular Army, the Regiment was reduced from three to two battalions, the 1st and 2nd; and so it remains.

That is our Regiment of Guards. It is a body of men whose detailed organisation has changed – and will no doubt change again – from time to time, but essentially the same as in the beginning, and with an unbroken tradition. It has never been disbanded. The soldiers who join it today learn their trade from older men who have probably experienced many of the 'little wars' of which we shall read, that have marked the period since the end of the Second World War. Those older men were instructed by veterans of the Second World War, whose commanders, when they themselves joined the Regiment, had served in the trenches and the great battles of the War of 1914–18. So it goes on, unbroken, one generation learning from another and teaching the next, passing on and developing new skills, but also passing on traditions, customs and privileges. So it goes on back through Londonderry, Malaya, Anzio, the Somme, through Africa, Inkerman, Waterloo; through Dettingen, Blenheim and Tangier, to that day in 1656 when King Charles II, a King temporarily and tragically in exile, entrusted to Thomas, Lord Wentworth the Colonelcy of a new personal Regiment of Guards to be formed at Bruges in Flanders: The Royal Regiment of Guards.

Early Days

BATTLE HONOURS*

Tangier, 1680 Namur, 1695

In 1656, Charles II had many loyal men around him. Oliver Cromwell ruled in England, an England increasingly dissatisfied with the dictatorial and puritanical regime of the Commonwealth. In 1658, Cromwell died and in 1660, General Monk marched on London and declared that there should be once again 'a free Parliament'. Elections were held, and the country shown to be strongly Royalist. The dictatorship was at an end and the King returned, amid huge rejoicing, 'to enjoy his own again'.

The Royal Regiment of Guards had been left in Flanders at the Restoration for financial and political reasons and in 1661, King Charles raised a second Regiment of Guards, 'His Majesty's Foot Regiment of Guards' ; the Colonel was John Russell A few years later, however, the veterans who had formed his first companies at Bruges – the original 'Royal Regiment of Guards' – were brought over to England and amalgamated with Russell's Regiment to form the 'First Regiment of Guards' of twenty-four companies, of which the senior, or right flank company would be the King's own company; and so it has remained.

A company in those times consisted of about 100 private soldiers commanded by a Captain. In the Regiment's early days companies were dispersed on garrison duty throughout the strategic ports and

'Ramillies', from the watercolour by Richard Simkin.

points of the Kingdom. A number of companies, however, were invariably close to, and responsible for, the safety of the Sovereign, wherever he was.

Companies would be brought together for particular campaigns; or, in the largely maritime operations against the Dutch, would serve aboard His Majesty's ships as marines – a service recalled by the custom of the 3rd Battalion playing 'Rule Britannia' before the National Anthem at Tattoo. Many companies of the Regiment, and not only those which constituted the 3rd Battalion, saw sea service. Indeed the King's Company itself embarked on the Duke of York's flagship at the Battle of Sole Bay in 1672.

When assembled in larger bodies or 'battalions' companies of the Guards were often united regardless of Regiment, so that companies of the Royal Regiment of Guards formed a composite battalion with companies of the Coldstream Regiment of Guards in a campaign to restore order in the Virginian Colony of America in 1676, and in the defence of Tangier against Moorish raiders in 1680.

The appearance of troops massed for battle often had a significant effect on the enemy, and the more imposing the appearance the greater the effect. Furthermore, a body of men who felt themselves the best turned out soldiers in the field would acquire a sense of pride and superiority which would stand them in good stead in the face of the enemy. It was not until the campaigns under Wellington, a supremely practical soldier, and the influence of men like Sir John Moore came to be felt that the British soldier was equipped primarily for fighting rather than display.

Training was a matter of the use of the weapon – chiefly the smooth-bore musket – and the complex

*The Battle Honours above are borne on the Colours of the Regiment, the Colours being decked with wreaths of laurel on the anniversaries of those battles printed in capital letters.

matter of priming and loading it. Success also depended upon perfection in close order drill. In an age when the individual weapon had little power or accuracy in isolation, the field could only be won by men working together; moving, changing direction and pace, and altering their formation on words of command, and above all firing volleys exactly as ordered. Only a well-drilled and toughened body working as one, could be effective. The force which produced such a body was drill and discipline.

Discipline was strict and punishments harsh. Flogging could only be awarded by sentence of Court Martial, but these could be convened quickly and sentences of several hundred lashes were not uncommon. Floggings were administered, in both Army and Navy, with the cat-o'-nine-tails, a short whip with nine knotted leather lashes, laid on by Drummers. By modern standards such sentences seem barbarous. It must be remembered that without absolute obedience the military body could not function, and that it had to be rigidly implemented, since anything else would be futile. Discipline was also a matter of enforcing good administration by strict orders so that every rank knew exactly what his duties were.

Light Company soldier, from an original print published by S. W. Fores of Piccadilly, dated 12.8.1793. This soldier 'of the newly raised companies embarked to join the Duke of York at the Siege of Valenciennes' wears the round hat with bearskin crest and green plume, and a shortened coat.

The soldier would often be 'quartered' on a household in the town or village where his duty took him, and the householder received a flat-rate quartering fee. Proper care of soldiers, therefore, required not only observation of rules but firmness toward those who could find it only too easy to cheat him.

A Guardsman in the 18th Century was paid little, but was secure in his employment. He was perfectly drilled and expert with his weapon, and he considered himself part of an elite Corps which could outmarch and outfight any troops in Europe. He was subject to strict discipline and harsh punishments, but could have confidence that his rations would not be stolen, nor his pay denied, since he knew that everyone in the Regiment were bound by firm regulations.

The Struggle with France

BATTLE HONOURS

Gibraltar, 1704–5	EGMONT-OP-ZEE
BLENHEIM	CORUNNA
RAMILLIES	BARROSA
OUDENARDE	NIVE
MALPLAQUET	Peninsula
DETTINGEN	
LINCELLES	

The 18th Century was marked by Britain's long struggle with France. It began with a series of campaigns in the Low Countries under William III; by Queen Anne's reign the campaigns we associate with the first Duke of Marlborough had become the War of the Spanish Succession. Then came the War of Austrian Succession, 1740–48; and the Seven Years War, 1756–63. The nature of what we call the War of American Independence, 1776–83 was changed when France, unprovoked, declared war on Britain – for the first time without allies – and Britain faced perhaps the most serious

'The Light Company counter-attacking in the orchard at Hougoumont', from the watercolour by Richard Simkin. (By courtesy Guards Museum)

threat of invasion in her history. Fighting took place at sea and on land, in America, Canada, India and Europe, culminating in twenty years of near-continuous war with Revolutionary France and the First Empire.

In this short book there is no space for description of all the battles; instead, we will focus on some scenes in which the 1st Guards played a conspicuous part. We begin during Marlborough's campaigns, appropriately since he was not only one of the greatest masters of the Art of War, but also Colonel of the 1st Guards, the Regiment in which he had held his first commission as a young man. Four great victories of Marlborough are inscribed on the Colours of the First Guards – Blenheim (1704), Ramillies (1706), Oudenarde (1708) and Malplaquet (1709). Let us look at an action which took place in 1704, shortly before the battle of Blenheim, the storming of the Schellenberg hill fort on the river Danube led by the First Guards.

The troops had been marching all day and were very tired. Marlborough had information which suggested that he might be able to take the Schellenberg that evening, 2 July, although the Bavarians, allies of France, had strongly entrenched it. The same information showed him that he would have far greater difficulty in taking it later. To take it was essential to the further prosecution of his campaign. He ordered the attack.

The troops had to assault up hill, cross ditches which the enemy had dug in front of the breastworks they had built, and, throughout the advance cannon would be fired direct on the advancing columns. The attack would have to be pressed through this, over the breastworks, then the enemy engaged in hand-to-hand fighting. Marlborough concentrated a great mass of infantry on a narrow front to achieve this. Every soldier, beside his musket, carried a 'fascine', a bundle of sticks, to throw into the ditches in order to be able to march across them. These were held in the left hand and the muskets shouldered on the right arm. The advance up the hill began just before six o'clock in the evening. The troops moved forward out of the shelter of a protecting wood and into the open, cannon began firing from an enemy battery on the flank, inflicting heavy casualties. The advance continued. Then, a short distance only from the enemy breastworks, cannon and musketry fire was intensively opened from the objective, the Schellenberg itself. Great gaps were torn through the ordered ranks. The enemy musket fire which poured into the advancing British Infantry from a range of a few yards was described as greater than any man had previously experienced. The attack slackened, Bavarians leaped out from the breastworks to counter-attack, and panic began among the attackers.

The 1st Guards lost all their senior officers and about half their men. They re-formed, faced the counter-attack and drove the Bavarians back to their trenches. Desperate hand-to-hand fighting took place for over an hour on the parapet, but eventually the assault failed, with a loss of about three thousand men. Marlborough ordered a second attack, then a third, and ultimately the place was taken by the combined efforts of the Allies.

Forty years later, during the War of Austrian Succession, at the Battle of Fontenoy, the British Infantry, with the First Guards on the right, advanced towards a much stronger body of French deployed behind a ridge. As they marched over the ridge they found themselves faced by their French equivalents – the French Guards, to their immediate front. The Captain of the King's Company stepped forward towards the enemy and invited them, in French, to fire first, expressing the hope that they would 'stand better' than they had at Dettingen in 1743. According to *The Regimental History*:

'"I hope, gentlemen", he shouted, "that you are going to wait for us today and not swim the Scheldt as you swam the Main at Dettingen". Then he turned to his own Company and said, "Men of the King's Company, these are the French Guards and I hope you are going to beat them today". The Company gave a cheer, and, after what was described as a half-hearted reply, French commands rang out. "For what we are about to receive may the Lord make us truly thankful", muttered a Guardsman, looking at the levelled French muskets thirty yards' away.'

The French, however, were surprised and shaken; their volley was ineffectual. The First Guards marched forward and delivered perfectly disciplined volleys at point-blank range and destroyed their opponents in a matter of minutes; then they marched on in good order. The British Infantry destroyed three Regiments of the French Guards and shattered three more Regiments of the Second Line by disciplined fire and order of their manoeuvres.

In 1756, yet another war with France began, the Seven Years War. The First Guards marched and counter-marched all over North Germany, against superior French forces, while in Canada the French were being driven from their possessions and the British American Empire was increasing rapidly. The final chapter in this 18th-Century struggle with France started as the war in America which led to the formation and independence of the United States. Initially the war in which the First Guards sent a contingent to form part of a

Two fine contemporary examples of full dress of members of the Grenadier Company. The officer (left) is Captain H. Wynyard, c. 1800, after a watercolour by H. Edridge. The Sergeant is J. Skinner, c. 1809, after a print in The Guards Museum, London.

composite body of Foot Guards, was purely against American Colonists, and the Guards took part with success in several battles and occupied Philadelphia. But after the declaration of war by France, Britain found herself isolated and her Navy overstretched. The Fleet had simultaneously to protect our lifeline to the Army in America, to keep the West Indies secure from French invasion (British possessions in these islands produced a large proportion of the national income) and to control the Channel to prevent invasion of Britain herself. The situation was too unpromising to be sustained, and when a British Army surrendered at Yorktown, the war, as far as the Guards were concerned, was over. Peace and the United States emerged.

The century was not wholly occupied by foreign wars. The privilege of mounting guard on the Sovereign, with a ceremony which has always taken place, continued throughout. There was no police force in England and duties in aid of the civil power could only be entrusted to the Army. The most serious of such incidents in which the Regiment was involved were the 'Gordon Riots' of 1780, in London. The First Guards (3rd Battalion) had to fire on a mob, and dominate the streets to prevent anti-Catholic crowds assembling.

In 1793, the French Revolutionary Government declared war on Britain and her Allies on the Continent. The wars which were thus begun took many forms and saw many shifts of Alliances during the next twenty-two years of almost continuous campaigning on land and sea. The only constant factors were the implacable hostility of Britain to a Continent dominated by France, and the determination to restore stability, which would be achieved by balance rather than conquest. So the 18th Century ended as it had begun: in a great contest with France, but this time it was with a France filled with new and Revolutionary fervour, and soon to be led by Napoleon Bonaparte.

These wars lasted, almost without interruption, from 1793 until 1815, but it will be impossible to do more than describe some of the epic scenes in which the First Guards participated. The Guardsman was still the well-drilled, strictly-disciplined, highly-trained and well-administered man his predecessors had been.

There had been changes in organisation. In the American War of Independence the usefulness of 'light companies' had been demonstrated, companies taught to skirmish, act more independently, and, as weapons improved, to act as individual marksmen. A Battalion consisted of one, sometimes two, Grenadier Companies and Light Companies. The remaining companies, of varying number dependent on the strength of the battalion were known as 'Battalion Companies'. Sometimes Grenadier or Light Companies were grouped together with similar companies of other battalions or Regiments to make a special force for a particular task.

Lord Saltoun, c. 1827, in the uniform of a field officer. He commanded a battalion in the defence of Hougoumont during the battle of Waterloo.

Each Battalion had a Corps of Drums, a Drum and Fife Band, to whose music it invariably marched, and who beat calls marking drill movements, 'Tattoo', announcing Reveille, particular duties or assembly for parade (bugle and bugle calls for this purpose were a much later innovation). In addition, the Regiment raised its own Regimental Band, based on London, which by convention, recruited a number of negroes. When a Battalion moved, or embarked on active service, it would be accompanied by an authorised number of wives who, apart from being on the 'ration strength' had no alternative but to march where their men marched, often doing laundry and repairs for most of the Battalion, sharing its sufferings and subjected to the same harsh punishments as their menfolk if they committed a crime.

In 1808, near the outset of the Peninsular War, Northern Spain saw one of the longest, most arduous, and ultimately successful campaigns ever fought by the British Army. An army under Sir John Moore had advanced from Portugal into Spain, and another force under Sir David Baird had landed at Corunna in Northern Spain and was ordered to march south-east into the interior to join Moore, together they were to threaten communications between France and the formidable French Army which had invaded and occupied Spain. The junction of forces took place; but French superiority was such that the British Army had no alternative but a long withdrawal to Corunna in the face of a fierce pursuit. Indeed this retreat had been anticipated by Moore, and supplies had been dumped along the route. It was by now mid-winter. On Christmas Day the retreat began.

The First Guards (1st and 3rd Battalions) had landed with Baird's force at Corunna. Now they took part in a retreat during which, owing to the frightful conditions of winter, the shortage of provisions and shelter and the incessant harassment by the French, discipline in parts of the Army broke down badly. Men deserted to take shelter; the discovery of wine led despairing men to drunkenness. The fighting power and the hopes of survival diminished.

No such instances were reported in the First Guards. Their discipline and *esprit de corps* kept them marching, fit to fight at all times. When on one occasion Moore halted the Army in order to fight a delaying action, the French attack, an attempt to turn the flank of the British withdrawal, was decisively defeated by the First Guards Battalions. Finally Corunna, the port of embarkation, came in sight. As the troops, utterly exhausted, marched towards the town, Moore watched and saw something encouragingly different and distinctive in the columns. 'Look at that body of men in the distance,' he said to his Staff, 'they are the Guards by the way they are marching.' The Guards Division, as it later became, was to uphold this unrelenting standard of discipline throughout the six years of hard campaigning that followed. As Wellington gradually matched, then forced onto the defensive, and finally smashed French power in the Peninsula, the senior formation in his splendid army was always composed of the Guards. Ultimately the Peninsular War ended with the successful invasion of France, and 'Peninsular' is one of the proudest of the Regiment's Battle Honours. Napoleon abdicated, and was confined to the Island of Elba.

Waterloo

BATTLE HONOURS
WATERLOO

In March 1815, Napoleon escaped and landed in France. Veterans of the Imperial Army rallied to him. The Allied Powers agreed on a grand strategy – a concerted advance on France from north and east. In the north an Allied Army, consisting of British, Netherland and Hanoverian contingents, under the Duke of Wellington, were deployed in Belgium and co-ordinated plans were made with a Prussian Army under Marshal Blucher.

The Army was quartered all over Belgium, able to concentrate on whatever direction proved to be necessary. The First Guards (2nd and 3rd Battalions) comprised the 1st Brigade of Guards and were stationed at Enghien, Hove and Marcq in Flanders. The previous weeks had been busy with concentration, administration and reviews; the

'On route for the Crimea, 1854', after a watercolour by Richard Simkin.

'The Roll Call', from an oil painting by Lady Butler, depicting the survivors of the detachment of the 3rd Battalion after the successful withdrawal from the Sandbag Battery at the battle of Inkerman. The mounted officer is Captain, later General, Sir George Higginson. When the 3rd Battalion of the Regiment was placed in suspended animation on 31st March, 1961, Her Majesty The Queen directed that a composite company should be formed from all ranks of the 3rd Battalion and should become the Left Flank Company of the 2nd Battalion in order to keep alive the traditions of the 3rd Battalion. Her Majesty directed that this new Company should be known as The Inkerman Company. The Company Call of The Inkerman Company is the former 3rd Battalion Call. (National Army Museum)

latter had involved much marching and exertion in hot weather. The troops were fit. There had been racing and cricket matches, and the return to active service after the short peace of 1814 was welcomed by many. There were grumbles, some with a familiar ring. 'In the Guards we subalterns have one great disadvantage: that most of the Generals choose their ADCs amongst us, so that the Regimental Subaltern Officer has to do double duty!'

It was anticipated that Napoleon would seek to destroy one enemy and then turn to face another, and his invasion of Belgium was thus confidently expected. The direction of his attack might be one of several. In the event he crossed the frontier from France on the night of 14 June, and at dawn on 15 June was already attacking the Prussians south of the river Sambre. The point of initial attack was now clear although it was some time before it could be clear to Wellington that it was also the only attack. On 16 June he marched from Brussels to intercept the French.

Spirits were high, as every British soldier had complete faith in the Allied Commander-in-Chief, and was convinced that even though the French were commanded by the great Napoleon, the Iron Duke would inflict on the French yet another – and they hoped, final – defeat.

The march was hot, the day sultry. There were no stragglers from either Battalion, and the men ceaselessly sang a popular song with the refrain 'All the world's in Paris'. At 3 p.m., very tired, the two battalions reached Nivelle hoping to rest but were again ordered forward to Quatre Bras. They had marched for 26 miles in intense heat. Officers dismounted and fell in, the senior Subaltern and junior Ensign of each Battalion, as was customary, took the King's and Regimental Colours respectively from the Colour Sergeants.

The 1st Brigade of Guards had marched to Quatre Bras preceded by the brigaded Light Companies of both Battalions. At about 5 o'clock these reached the Bois de Bossu north of the Quatre Bras cross roads, and were deployed into the wood to drive the French out. As successive companies came up, they were ordered into the wood to support the Light Companies who were invisible through the trees. In the confusion inseparable from this sort of situation, the Light Companies themselves suffered considerable loss from the fire of their own comrades, as well as from accurate heavy artillery fire which the enemy brought to bear upon the wood.

The wood was ultimately cleared, and both Battalions emerged from it, formed line, and repeatedly attacked the enemy. A French Cavalry counter-attack was routed, after the 2nd Battalion's left flank had again sought the cover of the wood; by nightfall both battalions had inflicted great punishment on the enemy and were in possession of the field, but at considerable cost. In reading of the epic performance of the 1st Guards two days later it should be remembered that their ranks had been depleted by over 500 casualties on the field of Quatre Bras.

During 17 June the Army withdrew. The 1st Guards marched at mid-day, the weather was heavy and showery. The night was spent on the northern slopes of a sharp ridge, north of the Manor of Hougoumont. An officer of the 3rd Battalion wrote: 'We piled arms and laid down in a wet ploughed field in a rut of water, when I found my mackintosh cloak anything but water-proof! Not allowed to light fires until daylight, around which we huddled, with shaking and clapping of teeth'. It rained all night.

For the Light Companies of the 1st Guards the night had been not only wet but busy. Joined by the Light Companies of the Coldstream and 3rd Guards, they had been ordered to prepare Hougoumont for defence; and barricading of gates, loopholing of walls and entrenching were set in hand. French patrols made contact with the 1st Guards' picquets in Hougoumont orchard during the night, but were driven off.

The part played by the 1st Guards at Waterloo on Sunday 18 June 1815 falls into three main phases. First, the defence of Hougoumont by the Light Companies. Second, the reception and repulse of massed cavalry attacks with which Napoleon sought to break the Allied centre, and third, the defeat of the Imperial Guard. In addition, and accompanying or between these phases of the action, the Regiment was exposed to sustained artillery fire and close range musketry of French skirmishers who infiltrated up to the main position.

Fresh troops, principally German, were sent to reinforce Hougoumont in the morning; and by what may have been a misunderstanding the Light Companies of the 1st Guards were withdrawn to join their battalions, reaching the ridge where they were posted at about the time the first French attacks on Hougoumont by Jerome Bonaparte began the battle of Waterloo.

There was a cry on the ridge, 'The Nassauers are driven out of the orchard, Light Companies to the front', and the Light Companies charged down the hill to counter-attack. Fighting with the other two

'Private Palmer winning the Victoria Cross', from an original oil painting.

Light Companies of the Guards, they eventually drove the French from the orchard.

Throughout the first part of the battle, Hougoumont was the scene of incessant fighting. It was the key to the Allied right flank, exposing an advancing or encircling enemy to enfilade fire on his flank. The Coldstream and 3rd Guards Companies were responsible for the house and buildings. The 1st Guards fought chiefly in the orchard. Eventually reinforcements, consisting first of additional companies of the 3rd Guards and later of the entire 2nd Brigade of Guards were deployed to Hougoumont and the companies of the 1st Guards were withdrawn, having suffered very severe losses. 'The survivors of the Light Companies', wrote an officer, 'joined their Battalions just before the charges of cavalry.'

While the battle had been raging at Hougoumont the remaining companies of the Regiment had found what shelter they could from the enemy's incessant and accurate artillery fire by lying down and by using, to its limited best, the cover of a wall and ditch which ran across their position.

Now followed the most formidable of tests, in imagination, if not in reality, for a cavalry attack offered no serious threat to an unbroken infantry square. The mass of 4,000 cavalry, which attacked the British centre, charged up to, around, and past the squares of Infantry, appearing to dominate the field, threatening each square on every side.

'Crossing the Alma, 1854', from the watercolour by Richard Simkin.

Although the French tried in vain, and with courage, to draw fire in order to create an opportunity of charging defenceless men, the controlled, disciplined musketry of the 1st Guards, formed into squares four ranks deep, did great execution.

As evening approached, the two days' fighting and marching began to be felt by the troops. Casualties had been heavy. The Light Companies at Hougoumont; the losses at Quatre Bras; the enemy's earlier attacks and incessant cannonade had all taken severe toll. The 2nd and 3rd Battalions were tired, stunned and very depleted when they were again ordered to form from square to line and lie down behind the ridge. 'Ordered to lie down, and so fatigued were we that some of my men were snoring fast asleep.'

The sleep was short. The movement into line was hardly completed when the enemy artillery fire stopped, the smoke cleared, and up the southern slopes of the ridge came three Regiments of the Infantry of the French Imperial Guard; a fresh force 5,000 strong, concealed hitherto in a fold of ground. To British soldiers lying down behind the ridge the chief impression was the sound of tramping feet, the vibration of the earth to the disciplined French advance, as yet unseen.

The French deployed as they reached the crest; and there arose from the ground to their immediate front, at twenty paces distance, the two battalions of the 1st Guards. The upshot is well known. Let a survivor relate it:

'Up came the brave Duke calling out to us, "Now Guards at them again.": and what did we behold, a large mass creeping up the declivity "en Bataillon serée", fine stout fellows with huge fur Grenadier caps, screaming out 'Vive l'Empereur, en avant, en avant". We formed a line of four deep, the first rank kneeling, the second also firing, the third and fourth loading and handling on to the front, and kept up such a continuous fire into the mass of heaped up Grenadiers who were also taken in flank by General Adam's Brigade . . . and this was the bouquet to all slaughter!'

Thus ended Waterloo and the Napoleonic wars.

To the 1st Guards, as to every Regiment who fought that day, Waterloo is a name of dramatic power. The battle brought to an end a long war, and a legend of Napoleonic invincibility. The Emperor himself, for the first time, encountered the greatest of British Captains, and lost. The Imperial Guard, fresh and in full regimental strength, put out a powerful part of its force in assault on the British Guards, and was thrashed, despite the weakness and exhaustion of the latter.

In honour of this victory the following order was published on 29 July 1815:

'In the name of the King, HRH The Prince Regent has been pleased to approve that the Regiment should henceforth be made a Regiment of Grenadiers and styled "The First or Grenadier Regiment of Foot Guards" in commemoration of their having defeated the Grenadiers of the French Imperial Guards at Waterloo."'

Thus all companies of the Regiment adopted the bearskin cap, white plume, and the Grenade badge; and wear it to this day.

Victorian Wars

BATTLE HONOURS

ALMA	Suakin, 1885
INKERMAN	KHARTOUM
SEVASTOPOL	MODDER RIVER
TEL-EL-KEBIR	South Africa, 1899–1902
Egypt, 1882	

A long European peace followed Waterloo. It was, however, disturbed forty years later by the ambitions of Russia. Meanwhile the usual reductions and economies which tend to mark a long peace took place. The Duke of Wellington became Colonel of the Regiment in 1827. It can, therefore, be said that Britain's two greatest soldiers, Marlborough and Wellington, was each in his time Colonel of the First Guards.

In 1854 the Crimean War broke out, and an expedition was assembled to be sent to the Crimean Peninsula in the Black Sea. After some weeks in Malta, the First Guards (3rd Battalion) sailed as part of a Guards Brigade for the Dardenelles. Three months, from June to September, were spent at Varna on the Black Sea, and on 14 September the Army landed on the Crimean Peninsula, and within days fought the Battle of Alma, crossed the river and drove the Russians back to the fortress of Sevastapol, which became the object of a long siege.

On the heights of Inkerman on the morning of 5 November 1854, a huge Russian column emerged from Sevastopol to break into and outflank the British right, and to break up the organised siege. The battle which ensued was fought in a mist, which made cohesion and control difficult for both sides. It was a day of regimental officers and for soldiers rather than for manoeuvres of High Command; and it was one of the hardest and most gruelling battles the Regiment has ever fought.

Sergeant Major Gubbins, 2nd Battalion, 1856. He wears the double-breasted tunic introduced in 1855; note the special NCO's sword, and the coat of arms superimposed on four gold chevrons.

Desperate fighting dominated by the bayonets of the Grenadiers centred round the taking and retaking of the Sandbag Battery, from which the Russians had driven a British picquet at the start of the engagement.

The only Colours in the Army carried that day were those of the 3rd Battalion. Passed from hand to hand, regardless of rank, they were the rallying point for a part of the battalion cut off in the Sandbag Battery and isolated from the rest of their Division. The detachment, about a hundred Grenadiers, fought their way back through a mass of Russians, all bent on the capture of the precious symbols of a British Regiment's life. The Adjutant, Captain Higginson, later General Sir George Higginson, described the scene:

'Clustered round the Colours, with scarcely a round of ammunition left, the men pressed slowly backwards, keeping their front full towards the enemy, their bayonets ready at the "charge". As a comrade fell, wounded or dead, his fellow took his place and maintained the compactness of the gradually diminishing group that held on with unflinching stubbornness in protecting the flags. More than once from the lips of this devoted band of non-commissioned officers and rank-and-file came the shout, "Hold up the Colours!" fearing, no doubt, that in the mist and smoke they might lose sight or touch of those honoured emblems, which they were determined to preserve, or in their defence to die. The two young officers, Verschoyle and Turner, raised them well above their heads, half unfurled, and in this order we moved slowly back, exposed to fire, fortunately desultory and ill-aimed, from front, rear, and left flank. Happily the ground on our right was so precipitous as to deter the enemy from attempting to outflank us on that side. As from time to time some Russian soldiers, more adventurous than their fellows, sprang forward towards

Drum Major Goddard, 1855. He joined the regiment in 1842 and fought at Alma, Balaclava, Inkerman and Sevastopol; he was awarded the Turkish Crimean Medal and The Meritorious Conduct Medal, and left the Regiment in 1869. Note the simulated double-breasted front to the tunic; this was in fact single-breasted and fastened by hooks and eyes.

our compact group, two or three of our Grenadiers would dash out with the bayonet and compel speedy retreat. Nevertheless, our position was critical. By the time, however, we had traversed half the distance to the breastworks of the Second Division (which I proved by subsequent measurement to be 700 yards distant from the Sandbag Battery), the pressure on our rear and left was relaxed, the Russian column having been sternly repulsed by the force occupying the ridge; while our men welcomed with a cheer a company of Zouaves bringing up at last on our right the timely aid which General Bosquet had, no doubt for sufficient reasons, been prevented from sending earlier. The enemy on our immediate front soon realised the danger of a further advance and fell back. Free at length to rejoin our main body, we hastened our pace, and soon descried the Duke of Cambridge and the rest of our Brigade on the crest of the ridge. I shall never forget the cheer with which the returning Colours were welcomed by all ranks; HRH being almost moved to tears for, as they all said, "We had given you up for lost." Many a time have my thoughts flown back over the waste of years to this stirring episode; many a time I have told the story among friends; never until now have I ventured to commit it to writing; for, indeed, my pen would have failed at any time in an attempt to impress a reader with the varying emotion which filled my mind while the safety of our Colours was in jeopardy. The mere possibility of the Colours of the First Regiment of our Sovereign's Guards being laid as a trophy at the feet of the Czar had to be faced, and I believe that a prayer went up from all of us that such dishonour might be averted at all costs. Certainly the grave faces and resolute attitude of our Grenadiers made me realise that there was no exaggeration in the language used by Sir William Napier in his well-known description of the behaviour of the 1500 British soldiers, all who remained to stand triumphant on the fatal hill at Albuera – "None know with what majesty the British soldier fights."

'Time has not served to dim my respect and

Captain Verschoyle, 1856; as an ensign he carried one of the Colours at the withdrawal from the Sandbag Battery, Inkerman.

Two pioneers: left, Pioneer Sergeant Robinson, 1961, and right, Pioneer Gillard, 2nd Battalion, 1856.

admiration for the bravery and devotion of this little group of Grenadiers in the defence of their Colours on the day of Inkerman. The tattered fragments of those Colours have found their final resting place on the walls of the Guards' Chapel. I feel confident that none of my readers is so cynical as to smile if I admit that I never enter that treasure-house of memorials, so dear to every member of the Brigade of Guards, and feel able to gaze without emotion on the Colours which served as our rallying point on the dark upland of Inkerman.'

The first Victoria Crosses were awarded in the Crimean War, four of them to Grenadiers of the 3rd Battalion.

The remainder of 19th-Century British history was dominated by small wars, as the Empire enlarged and consolidated. The 2nd Battalion took part in the expedition to Egypt in 1882 crowned by the victory of Tel-El-Kebir. The 1st Battalion – as a single Guards Battalion, not forming part of a Guards Brigade – formed part of Lord Kitchener's expedition to reconquer the Sudan which culminated in the Battle of Omdurman.

Great changes and improvements came about in the administration of the Army. Flogging was abolished. New barracks were built in military cantonments in various parts of the country, and married soldiers, for the first time, had the prospect

Lt-Colonel Henry Ponsonby photographed in winter clothing in Canada, 1863. The 1st Battalion were sent to Canada in 1862 to help guard the U.S. border during the American Civil War.

of a 'married quarter'; hitherto his only privacy had been a blanket hung across a corner of the barrack room. New barracks had central cook-houses from where food would be brought by orderlies to each barrack room and eaten on the barrack-room table, the Picquet Officer being required to visit each barrack room in turn to see whether there were any complaints before the meal was concluded.

Both the 2nd and 3rd Battalions of the Grenadiers, although not brigaded together, took part in the South African War. This was a war of marching and counter-marching, the manning of block-houses and 'stop lines' as elusive Boer Commandos were gradually confined and their brilliant mounted exploits contained and prevented. In the earlier stages there had been pitched battles of a more recognisable type. One such was at Belmont where, as part of the 1st Division, and fighting in a Guards Brigade with two Battalions of the Coldstream and one Battalion of the Scots Guards, the advancing British found their route to the north, towards Kimberley, barred by 2,000 Boers, well deployed and largely concealed in a chain of small rocky hills rising from the veldt. It was necessary to carry out a frontal attack across open ground in daylight, an operation which, while the norm in previous ages, was becoming an increasingly disagreeable manoeuvre in the face of modern small-arms fire, the Boers being expert marksmen. Nevertheless, the Grenadiers doubled across the ground, climbed the rocky slopes, and drove the Boers from their positions with the bayonet.

The principal effect of the South African War, however, was the impetus it gave to reform in the Army. New weapons, new uniforms, a new organisation at the top, and the formation of the Territorial Army were combined with the creation of an Expeditionary Force for any future European War. Hitherto, Britain had improvised the creation of armies when crisis arose. Now she was determined to have at least the leading elements already created.

RECIPIENTS OF THE VICTORIA CROSS

The Crimean War

Colonel The Hon H. H. M. Percy
Brevet Major Sir Charles Russell Bt
Sergeant A. Ablett
Private A. Palmer

The 1914–18 War

Captain and Brevet Major (Acting Lt-Colonel) Viscount Gort MVO DSO MC
Lieutenant (Acting Captain) G. H. T. Paton MC
Lieutenant (Acting Captain) T. T. Pryce MC
Lance-Sergeant J. H. Rhodes DCM
Lance-Corporal W. D. Fuller
Private E. Barber
Private W. E. Holmes

The 1939–45 War

Major The Hon W. P. Sidney
Lance-Corporal H. Nicholls

The First World War

BATTLE HONOURS

MARNE, 1914	ARRAS, 1918
AISNE, 1914	HAZEBROUCK
YPRES, 1914, '17	HINDENBURG LINE
LOOS	FRANCE & FLANDERS, 1914–18
SOMME, 1916, '18	
CAMBRAI, 1917, '18	

The Great War against Germany took a heavier toll of the British Army than any before or since. It did not last as long as the Peninsular War, or the Second World War. It was, as far as land fighting was concerned, largely confined to one theatre, France and Flanders, although there were 'side-shows', often very tragic and expensive, like Gallipoli and Mesopotamia. For the mass of the British Army and for the Grenadiers' four battalions (a fourth was formed in 1915) the war meant the Western Front.

It was a war which started and finished with a great deal of marching and manoeuvre, as, in 1914, the great German encircling movement through Belgium drove back the Allied left wing, including the British Expeditionary Force, and finally stopped at the Battle of the Marne. Four years later the German front finally collapsed and in a series of brilliant victories the Allies brought them to surrender. In the four years between the opening and closing phases the number of troops employed by both sides was so huge, so evenly balanced, that the entire front, from neutral Switzerland to the sea, was the scene of a bloody and exceptionally muddy stalemate.

The war thus became very largely a matter of trench, dug-out and barbed wire, with opposing trenches often very close to each other. The trench systems were continuous. They were dug in depth, with support trenches forming successive lines; and were supplied by communication trenches up which reinforcements and supplies moved, and back through which wounded were evacuated. It was the constant task of battalions to maintain trenches, revet walls against collapse, to clean, wage constant war against rats and repair the damage created by enemy shell and mortar fire. At

A splendid photograph of a group of NCOs, about 1870. (National Army Museum)

Officers of the 3rd Battalion at Suakin, Sudan, 1884/5. The early pattern tropical tunics are cut in similar style to the Norfolk jacket. (Institute of Royal Engineers)

night, from the trenches, patrols would creep into No Man's Land to gather information, recover wounded men, or carry out raids to gain prisoners and identify the enemy opposite. From the trenches, working parties crawled out to repair our own wire. All the time men were exposed to damp, lice and enemy shell fire; while snipers were quick to pick off any head unwisely raised above the parapet.

This disagreeable life could not be sustained for many days at a time without troops becoming stale, after a few days a battalion would be relieved and spend some time 'out of the line' in rest billets; then the trenches again.

The stalemate, however, was taking place on Allied territory; the German trench line ran across France and Belgium, and behind it Allied territory, including the Belgian capital, Brussels, was occupied by the German Army and subject to the Military Administration. It was thus a situation in which political pressures alone made Allied offensive necessary. Nor was this all. Each part of the front had its effect on every other part, since an attack in one sector forced the defenders to concentrate and to weaken other sectors. The response to this might have to be a counter-attack in some other sector to take the pressure off another part of the front. Thus, for instance, the great German attacks at Verdun in 1916, where large parts of the German and French armies bled nearly to death in the struggle, made absolutely imperative an Allied effort that summer in another sector. The sufferings of the French at Verdun meant that the Battle of the Somme had to be begun by the British Army in July and no later. There were many such campaigns. Inaction was not a possible option for the Allies however difficult and costly the offensive tended to be.

There were organisational changes about this time, to which the Grenadiers contributed, and which have particularly marked the 20th-Century history of the Regiment.

First, because of the magnificent performance of the Irish Regiments in South Africa it was decreed by Queen Victoria that a Regiment of Irish Guards be formed to enlarge the Household Troops. Some 75 Grenadiers, of all ranks, were selected to form the basis of a new Regiment. In 1915 the Welsh Guards were created. This was of particular significance for the Grenadiers, since Wales had long been a Grenadier recruiting area, providing many of the senior members of all Grenadier Battalions. The Grenadiers, therefore, provided 640 men for the new Regiment and maintained with it a particularly close affinity.

It has always been a tradition of the Household Troops, from earliest times, to form composite bodies or Corps from several or all Regiments if the demand exists. In Africa a Guards Camel Corps had been formed. In the war of 1914–18 a Guards Machine Gun Battalion was created; and in more recent times we have seen a Guards Parachute Battalion and Company, and a Guards Special Air Service Squadron to name but a few.

Lastly, it had always been customary to group battalions of Foot Guards together on active service in 'Guards Brigades'; in the Napoleonic Wars such brigades had on occasion been grouped in the same Division of the Army, as at Waterloo. In August 1915, a Guards Division was formed concentrating all battalions of the Guards into one elite formation on the Western Front – three brigades, each of four battalions, under the command of the Earl of Cavan, himself a Grenadier.

Specific mention should be made of the part played by the Grenadiers in October/November 1914 in the battle known as 'First Ypres', a battle in which it has been said that the old British Regular Army died. After the first great German offensive of the war had been halted on the Marne and pushed back to the River Aisne each side moved, as rapidly as possible, to encircle the opponent's northern flank since a stalemate was already developing inland. This movement by both Allies and Germans became known as 'the race to the sea'. As far as the Allies were concerned it was the most 'close-run thing' since Waterloo, but in the face of great German superiority it was clear that the battle would end in the defensive – and the defensive against odds. A line was created and it just held.

The 1st Battalion, Grenadiers, found themselves the left battalion of the 7th Division, while their neighbours were other Guardsmen of the 1st Guards Brigade standing in front of Ypres. Against this junction new German Divisions attacked repeatedly without success. In the mists of early morning on 29 October 1914, 'standing to' in hurriedly-dug individual trenches, the Grenadiers saw great masses of German Infantry moving behind their left rear, and were simultaneously attacked in front. They withdrew and refaced with part of the Battalion, and manned a ditch as well as support trenches dug behind them. The Germans attacked in mass formation, and fell by the hundred before the sustained and accurate British rifle fire. The Grenadiers launched two counter-attacks with the bayonet across open ground to clear the Germans from some lodgement they had gained. Ultimately, the Battalion withdrew to some brick-yards, and were able to reorganise. Out of 23 officers, 11 had been killed and 8 wounded, and in the brickyards the 1st Battalion found itself reduced to a strength of 4 officers and 100 men. A few days later they were temporarily organised as a single company.

The 2nd Battalion had similar experiences in the following few days of early November. The same massed German Infantry attacks, the same intensive shelling by all types of artillery and mortars. The 2nd Battalion was, at this time, moved from one division and brigade to another as different demands arose. On 11 November only 3 officers and 74 men were left. There had never before been comparable casualties. The established strength of each battalion was 900; but First Ypres, bloody though the fighting was, achieved at least its defensive aim. German encirclement of the Allied left wing was frustrated, and defeat avoided.

The battle of the Somme had opened on 1 July 1916; the Guards Division, which had not been involved in the earlier stages, was moved south to the Somme area in September taking part in the attack towards Flers on 15 September, the first action in which tanks were employed. After the battles of the 15/16th in which all four battalions of Grenadiers were committed there was a slight respite. Then, on 25 September, came the attack on Les Boeufs.

The extreme right of the Guards Division attack was taken by the 2nd Battalion; the extreme left by the 4th Battalion. It was necessary to cut through three lines of barbed wire in the open and charge to capture the enemy objective trench by bomb and bayonet. Thereafter, the advance was pushed by way of a sunken road into the shattered villages of Les Boeufs. The 1st Battalion moved through and captured the final objective. The Germans could be seen withdrawing over open country, their line was penetrated at last, although circumstances far beyond the control of Grenadiers rendered the victory inconclusive, it was nobly won. It had depended on careful preparation and practice before battle, on the leadership of officers and non-commissioned officers of all ranks, and on sheer disciplined courage and stubbornness of individual soldiers. Above all, perhaps, it had depended on the trust which all ranks had in each other, a sense of absolute unity in the Regimental family.

One last incident is worth describing. In facing the great, and nearly victorious, German offensive which began in March 1918, the 4th Battalion, on 13 April, found itself facing odds of over five to one as part of a greatly weakened 4th Guards Brigade. On the left flank No. 2 Company was isolated when the centre companies of the battalion were overrun. The Company was attacked from front, flank and

Corps of Drums, 1st Battalion, Gibraltar, 1897. The use of the white helmet is interesting.

Officers and men of the 2nd Battalion in South Africa during the Boer War, 1900.

rear, and drove back repeated attacks with unceasing rifle fire and a series of counter-attacks with the bayonet. With 17 men left and ammunition exhausted the Company Commander, Captain Pryce, finally charged the enemy. He had been seen, with his small group of survivors, engaged by enemy field guns at point-blank range. One survivor reported the occurrence, and a captured Grenadier officer was shown by the Germans the heaps of corpses in front of the post held by the intrepid No. 2 Company. Captain Pryce was awarded the V.C. posthumously for this exploit.

After the war of 1914–18 the Privates of the Guards were officially named 'Guardsmen'. No war before or since has brought more lustre to the title of 'Guardsman' or the name 'Grenadier'. The virtues which are inculcated in the Foot Guards from the start of their service – the importance of strict attention to detail, the vital nature of obedience to orders so that all take part, as limbs of a body, in a co-ordinated plan, and the supreme obligation of good administration and care for subordinates – were never better exemplified. Nor has higher courage or greater determination ever been demanded and shown.

After the Armistice the 1st Battalion was stationed in the United Kingdom until 1930, when they went to Egypt. They spent two years in the Middle East, then returned to the United Kingdom until the outbreak of war in 1939. The 2nd Battalion spent four years in the United Kingdom after 1918, then went to Constantinople, returning home one year later, where they remained until 1936, when the Battalion was posted to Egypt. They stayed in Egypt until 1937, then returned home. The 3rd Battalion stayed in France until 1919 then returned home, remaining on home station until 1933, when they went to Egypt, remaining in the Middle East until 1936 and returned to the United Kingdom until the outbreak of the war.

The Second World War

BATTLE HONOURS

DUNKIRK, 1940	ANZIO
MARETH	MONT PICON
MEDIJEZ PLAIN	GOTHIC LINE
SALERNO	NIJMEGEN
MONTE CAMINO	RHINE

Between the end of the First World War and the beginning of the Second much changed in the art of warfare. The First World War saw the emergence of the tank, as a slow-moving armour-protected gun crawling forward in support of infantry, and achieving much that had been hitherto impossible without great cost, in the context of static, positional warfare. Artillery shells turned battlefields into a quagmire. It was difficult to imagine another European war except in terms of the same sort of stalemate as that which had marked the Western Front; trenches, scrupulously observed routine, individual marksmanship. Furthermore, there was a general assumption that aerial bombardment would be so devastating that no nation could remain at war for long.

When the Second World War began, and above all when it erupted on the Western Front with the German offensive in France, Belgium and Holland in May 1940, it was clear that mechanization had brought about a great change. This change had been forecast and preached by the far-sighted; it first made general impact as a practical and actual method of waging war in the German offensives which came to be given the name 'Blitzkrieg'. The all-mechanised formation – tanks, mechanised infantry and command posts, supported by air power in lieu of heavy artillery – brought mobility to the battlefield once again. Great manoeuvres, almost inconceivable after the initial battles of 1914, were again witnessed, but now at a faster pace; the limiting factor was not the daily distance a man could march or a cavalryman ride, so much as the ability to supply vehicles with petrol and 'feed the advance'.

Yet this was only one aspect of the Second World War. Armoured operations could only be effective on certain terrain, parts of Europe, the Desert and Russia. In other theatres of operations the 'Blitzkrieg' was inappropriate; and in those theatres, or on that terrain, the infantryman, with the same skills as his father had required twenty-five years before, was the battle-winner. The infantry battalion transport, which had been horse-drawn until shortly before the Second World War, was now entirely motorised, although this was of dubious benefit in some of the mountain fighting, particularly in Italy, where supply was, and had to be, largely by mule.

Sergeants of the King's Company, 1904, wearing first pattern khaki field service dress introduced in 1902. The slouch hat was worn until the introduction of the peakless 'Broderick' cap shortly afterwards.

A study of a bugler of mounted infantry, England, c. 1905.

In the mountains of Italy or Eritrea, in the Burmese jungle, men needed to be able to march, shoot, dig and move on their feet by day and night with skill and endurance.

The most striking organisational change produced by the War was the formation of the Guards Armoured Division. It was decided in 1941 that more units of the Regular Army should be converted from Infantry to the Armoured role, and that a Guards Division should be formed. It was to be an Armoured Division, with some battalions of the Foot Guards converted to tank Battalions, others becoming mechanised Infantry, and the armoured reconnaissance elements to be formed from the Household Cavalry. A Guards Tank Brigade, originally units of the Guards Armoured Division, (including the 4th Battalion, Grenadiers, which had been re-formed in 1940), was detached as an independent formation to support infantry divisions.

Next must be mentioned the expansion of the Regiment. Not only the 4th Battalion, but, for the first time, a 5th and 6th Battalion were formed, and Guardsmen took a prominent part in the other specialist formations and units, notably Airborne and Commando, drawn from all Corps of the Army.

In terms of deployment, the Second World War was very different from the First, both for the British Army in general and the Regiment in particular. Whereas in the First War the Army had been overwhelmingly concentrated on the Western Front and all four Grenadier Battalions had formed part of the Guards Division, in the Second War Grenadier battalions fought in Western Europe, in the opening campaign of 1939–40 and in the closing and victorious campaign of 1944–45, in Italy, in the Western Desert, and in Tunisia. In consequence the experiences of Grenadiers were much more various and dissimilar in the Second War than in the First. Grenadiers who had joined at the Guards Depot together, early in the War and who survived, often met again at its conclusion feeling more strangers from each other than had been the case in the earlier war. Operations in various theatres had been so different from each other, memories were not the same.

For the Regiment the opening stage was the campaign of 1940, a great operational victory for the German Army. All three regular Battalions formed part of the British Expeditionary Force under the Commander-in-Chief, a Grenadier, Lord Gort. The main attack directed on the Franco-Belgian border with Germany was aimed at cutting the Allied forces in two; the British, the French left wing and the Belgians would, it was correctly calculated, have moved forward to meet a deliberately slower and less mechanised German advance in the North, and as they moved forward they would facilitate their own separation from the main body of the French Army in the South. For the Grenadiers it was a matter of hard defensive fighting and quickly mounted counter-attacks in a situation where uncertainty and despair became increasingly prevalent – and of withdrawing in good order.

The withdrawal ended in an evacuation, from Dunkirk to England. Throughout, the Grenadiers, as at Corunna 132 years before, were judged by all to have set a fine and much needed example of discipline amid a considerable measure of chaos. No arms were lost, and units kept their cohesion (the entire 3rd Battalion marched with precision to the harbour of Dunkirk and 'dressed' properly before embarkation). The tradition was maintained.

So varied and numerous were the battles fought by the battalions of the Regiment, as the list of Battle Honours testifies, that description must be selective. First, the Western Desert in March 1943: the 6th Battalion Grenadiers formed part of the 201st Guards Brigade in the 8th Army, advancing westward after the previous autumn's great victory of El Alamein to link hands with the Anglo-American forces which had invaded French North Africa. Their way was barred by a strong position known as the Mareth line in Southern Tunisia. Mareth was the 6th Battalion's first battle. The attack went in by night. It involved a long march across a 'wadi', or dry shallow valley in the desert, and the storming of what were believed to be lightly-held German positions on a low range of hills.

The battalion advance soon encountered a minefield. Large numbers of anti-personnel mines started to take their toll of the Grenadiers, and had been mixed with anti-tank minefields which made the movement of support vehicles and heavy weapons virtually impossible. Mine detection and mine-clearing took place in darkness, by hand.

The German position was strong; the night advance by-passed a large number of German posts which started brisk enfilade fire and fire from the rear on to the forward companies. Eventually they were withdrawn – an order hard to convey, and in some cases near impossible to execute. The fate of many officers and men was for some time uncertain, 14 officers were killed in this, the 6th Battalion's first battle, and in all some 280 casualties were inflicted. Admiration for the courage and skill of the Grenadiers' performance in appalling conditions was expressed by all, not least by the Germans themselves. The 6th Battalion, first to land in Italy, went from glory to glory in the bitter struggle northward up the Italian peninsular, but had no finer hour than in its first battle among the mines, cross-fire, and darkness of Mareth.

In January 1944, an Allied force was landed at Anzio on the west coast of Italy, behind the main south-facing front held by the Germans. The landing was successful but, for reasons which military historians will long debate, it was not exploited quickly, and the beachheads were sealed off and counter-attacked with ever increasing ferocity by the Germans. The 5th Battalion Grenadiers formed part of the Allied force. About ten days after landing, and having been continuously in action, the Battalion had its most

The King's Royal Regt of Foot Guards, 1685
1 Captain of Musketeers
2 Captain of Grenadier Company
3 Musketeer
4 Grenadier

ANGUS McBRIDE

A

The First Regiment of Foot Guards, 1704
1 Private, Grenadier Company
2 Officer, Battalion Company
3 Private, Battalion Company

B

ANGUS McBRIDE

The First Regiment of Foot Guards, 1792
1 Drummer
2 Sergeant, Grenadier Company
3 Officer, Battalion Company
4 Private, Battalion Company

ANGUS McBRIDE

D

ANGUS McBRIDE

The Grenadier Guards, 1854
1 Officer
2 Guardsman
3 Drummer
4 Colour Sergeant

ANGUS McBRIDE

E

F

ANGUS McBRIDE

The Grenadier Guards, 1914-45
1 Lieutenant, 1914
2 Guardsman, North Africa 1942-43
3 Guardsman, Guards Armoured Division, NW Europe 1944-45

ANGUS McBRIDE

The Grenadier Guards, 1970s
1 Captain Frockcoat Order
2 Regimental Sergeant Major, Full Dress
3 Guardsman Internal Security kit

H

ANGUS McBRIDE

savage trial. On the night of 7 February a triple German attack struck the Battalion holding a position behind Carroceto. At Battalion Headquarters it was unclear what exactly had happened to the three left and left front companies, except that they had been heavily attacked and might have been overrun. Suddenly a party of Germans appeared in the moonlight at the top of a deep gulley in which Battalion Headquarters and Support Company Headquarters were sited, some of them storming into the gulley itself. Had the few men at Headquarters been overrun the Germans could have cut off the rest of the battalion and, by opening a road running through the position, cleared the way for a German armoured advance to the beachhead base.

Support Company Headquarters became a fighting detachment. The Company Commander, Major Sidney, hurled grenades at the advancing Germans, and went on fighting after being himself wounded by a German grenade; the Germans withdrew, but the 5th Battalion's epic stand at Anzio cost them dear. In the continuous and dogged fighting throughout February 1944, the battalion lost 29 officers and 560 men – out of 800.

Lastly we turn our attention to a very different scene. In September 1944, the Guards Armoured Division formed the spearhead of the British Army advancing up one narrow road into Holland to link up with parachute and airlanded assaults delivered by the 1st Airborne Corps. These airborne operations had been delivered to seize key bridges over canals and the two great rivers, the Neder Rijn and the Waal, which, once crossed, would leave no major obstacle between the Allied Armies and North Germany. The object was to launch the Army up a narrow corridor, since German troops, undefeated, although in some areas disorganised, were both East and West of the corridor. The obstacles would have been taken by air assault. The last bridge was at Arnhem, objective of the 1st British Airborne Division; the other great bridge some twelve miles south was at Nijmegen, objective of the 82nd United States Airborne Division. The Guards Armoured Division entered Nijmegen on 19 September – the whole operation having started on 17th – to find that, after fierce fighting, the 82nd Airborne Division were still held up in the town and the bridge was in German hands. Meanwhile, although this was not clearly appreciated at the time, the 1st Airborne Division at Arnhem had encountered entirely unexpected German armoured troops and were fighting a desperate battle of survival, with one skeleton battalion hanging onto the north end of the Arnhem bridge and the Germans holding the south end.

An attempt to rush the Nijmegen bridge on the afternoon of 19 September had failed. Thereafter the town was methodically cleared by the 1st and 2nd Battalions in collaboration with the Americans. Strong German positions commanding southern approaches to the bridge were stormed by the King's Company and No. 4 Company of the 1st Battalion supported by tanks of the 2nd Battalion. At seven o'clock in the evening a small detachment of tanks of the 2nd Battalion rushed at the bridge, in spite of anti-tank fire and the knocking out of some of our tanks in the hazardous crossing the Grenadiers reached the other side, engineers quickly removed the demolitions, and the intact Nijmegen bridge was in Allied hands. American parachutists, meanwhile, had carried out an operation of outstanding courage, crossing the wide river in open assault boats some way to the west under enemy fire from the far bank, gaining a lodgement and exploiting eastward to link up with the armoured troops. Only one obstacle remained, the river at Arnhem. Tragically, the 1st Airborne Division were ground to pieces by overwhelming strength; German troops used the bridge to reinforce the ground, a highly defensible raised road with no opportunity to deploy tanks off it, between Arnhem and Nijmegen, and the great objective was not attained.

Casualties of Grenadiers in the Second World War were, in spite of six (smaller) battalions in the field, considerably less than those incurred between 1914 and 1918 on the Western Front – 4,500 against some 16,000. It must, however, be remembered that in the First War four battalions were incessantly active in France and Flanders for four long years; whereas in the Second World War, apart from the Dunkirk campaign of 1940, no battalion went into action until December 1942, and casualties were largely suffered in the last two years of war. Two V.C.s were awarded to the Regiment during the Second World War.

Statistics tell only a small part of the story, just as

we have illuminated only a tiny part of the Grenadiers' actions in the Second World War. Throughout the spirit of comradeship, loyalty to the idea of the Regiment, and pride in its achievements provided, in both World Wars, the inspiration which governed all.

The Post-War Years

Any period following a major war is generally marked by reductions of Armed Forces. It has also, too frequently, been marked by deterioration in training and fighting quality as recollection of experience fades, as less operational functions predominate, and as a general atmosphere prevails of – 'it can't happen again.'

The period between 1945 and the present day has unfortunately been no exception, insofar as the reductions of the British Army has been concerned. For the Grenadiers the blow has been particularly bitter. The 4th and 5th Battalions were disbanded after the war. The 6th Battalion had been disbanded before the end of the war, but not only the non-regular battalions were to suffer. In 1960 the 3rd Battalion of the Regiment held a farewell parade inspected by Her Majesty the Queen in the gardens of Buckingham Palace. The 3rd Battalion, which had a certain claim to be the oldest Battalion of the Regiment because of the origins of some of the Companies which originally composed it had a particular style and liveliness of spirit all of its own, and the Regiment was the poorer for its passing. Perhaps history, always unpredictable, will see its resurrection. However, Her Majesty the Queen decreed that a company to be known as the Inkerman Company should be transferred as the Left Flank Company of the 2nd Battalion, thus perpetuating the traditions of the old Battalion.

Three angles on a Colour Sergeant in Guard Order, 1910.

As to determination in fighting quality and the 'predominance of peacetime activities' the years since the Second World War, unlike most preceding post-war periods, have been marked by a succession of 'small wars' or warlike situations, not always coming under the heading of 'Internal Security', which have made these decades unique for Grenadiers. Battalions have served, fought, protected others, or trained in more parts of the world than ever before.

It started with the 3rd Battalion which, in the fifteen years of its life between the end of the Second World War and its disbandment, travelled more than any other. First, the Middle East; the end of the British Mandate in Palestine was a bitter period of struggle against two parties irreconcilable with each other, and the level of skill in terrorism and guerilla activity employed against the British Army in Palestine between 1945 and 1948 has seldom been surpassed. The 3rd Battalion handed over their duties in Palestine in May 1948 to the 1st Battalion, the latter witnessed the end of the British Mandate and, with the rest of the 1st Guards Brigade, were redeployed to Tripoli in Libya.

The 3rd Battalion had only spent a few months at Windsor on return (a period which coincided with the reintroduction of full dress for the Household Troops) when they were alerted for further duty in a theatre never before visited by a Grenadier Battalion, South-East Asia. In September 1948 they embarked in a troopship for Malaya as part of a hastily assembled 2nd Guards Brigade.

The Malayan emergency had broken out suddenly with a near-successful attempt by the Malayan Communist Party, almost entirely Chinese, to take over the country by a co-ordinated programme of industrial strife and armed terrorism in the plantation areas, all dependent on bases deep in the jungle. The enemy's operations were skilful

drawing on experience gained in fighting the Japanese Army. The 'Malayan Emergency' was protracted, but ultimately the campaign, containing a skilful amalgam of civil and military measures, was completely successful.

The Grenadiers took happily to the completely new task of jungle warfare. Operations included a good deal of straightforward guard duty, but the main attack technique was the deep jungle patrol, often lasting for days or weeks, wherein a company, moving through dense jungle by compass, would establish a base, patrol for information; or, acting on information, develop an offensive operation against a terrorist camp. Pre-requisites for success were careful planning, knowledge of how to survive in the jungle, quick marksmanship and physical endurance; the 3rd Battalion soon built up and maintained a reputation in all these attributes. Two years at home for the 3rd Battalion were followed by a further tour of duty in the Middle East. Initially the Battalion relieved the 1st Battalion in Tripoli in the summer of 1951; that winter there was trouble in the Canal Zone of Egypt where the British Army at that time maintained a considerable base, albeit only protected in peacetime by one brigade. The Egyptian Government announced its intention to abrogate the Anglo-Egyptian Treaty unilaterally. Disorders broke out in the Canal Zone itself. Soon the whole of the 1st Guards Brigade (and a further two divisions) found themselves moving to Egypt where a large Army was quickly established to maintain the British position while events in Egypt moved from revolution to revolution, until a long-term settlement could be arranged.

Drum Majors in Household Clothing or State Dress – c. 1830, 1856 and 1912. The present day dress is very similar to that worn at the beginning of this century.

In 1954 the 3rd Battalion was relieved by the 2nd Battalion and returned to London and Trooped the Colour in 1956. The respite was short. In August that year the 'Suez Crisis' led to the mobilisation of the Battalion by the recall of reservists, and its move, nearly 1,000 strong to Malta in anticipation of possible operations in Egypt. These finished before the Battalion was committed to them, yet instead of returning to England, the Battalion was sent to Cyprus where a full-scale emergency had broken out as a result of the EOKA terrorist movement launched in pursuit of the aim of

Interesting study of men of the 1st Battalion at Pirbright Camp in 1912; note the mixture of white Slade Wallace equipment and 1908 pattern khaki webbing.

ENOSIS: departure of the British, and union with Greece. The Turkish community, who had no intention of allowing this to happen, were initially peaceful though uneasy. Any moves by the British which could give credibility to the idea that ENOSIS might be granted were interpreted by the Turks as a direct threat; and soon intercommunal violence overlaid the comparatively straightforward anti-terrorist task.

The 3rd Battalion soon established a considerable reputation in the difficult, and skilful art of anti-terrorist operations in the face of potentially hostile propaganda and governed by strict political rules designed to prevent military action becoming politically counter-productive. Cyprus is very hot in summer and conditions of life and service were harsh. The 3rd Battalion returned to England in the autumn of 1959 and held their final parade in the summer of 1960. Since 1945 only one third of their service had been spent at home, the remainder on some sort of active service.

We have focused on one battalion, the 3rd, as an example of the life and service of Grenadiers in the post-war period. It was not unique. Often, as in Palestine and Egypt, the Battalion handed over its duties to another Battalion of the Regiment, whose experiences were similar. Often the 1st or 2nd Battalion would – on duties not unlike those already described – be deployed themselves to parts of the world previously unvisited by battalions of Grenadiers. In 1961 the 1st Battalion was sent as an independent force to what was then the British Southern Cameroon, where a civil war was being conducted on the frontier with a neighbouring territory, and where imminent independence following a United Nations sponsored plebiscite was causing a good deal of anxiety and fear for the future among the people. Spread over largely roadless jungle country or up country 'savannah' the companies of the Battalion were hundreds of miles apart, each responsible for a wild 'security zone' of huge extent and almost total independence. The Battalion withdrew the day after independence was finally granted.

In June 1963 the 2nd Battalion went for a nine month tour to British Guyana, the first Grenadier experience of South America. In 1973 the 2nd Battalion were sent for six weeks intensive training in British Honduras but tensions along the border with Guatemala extended that tour for nine months. A need for a British presence in the Persian Gulf resulted in the 1st Battalion serving at Sharjah from 1968 until 1969, and in addition No. 2 Company of the 2nd Battalion spent six months there with the Scots Guards during their tour in 1970. In recent years each of the 1st and 2nd Battalions have returned again and again for service in the tragic conditions of Northern Ireland.

There has been, however, another dimension to the Army's and the Regiment's preparedness for war. Since the Second World War the western nations have learned that unpreparedness leads not to peace but to a potential enemy gambling on our weakness to achieve swift victory, in other words to war. In order to prevent war, therefore, the watchword has been, 'keep sufficiently armed and alert'. Second, from the terrible experiences of the past we have learned that only in unity, in a combination of Allies demonstrating their will to help each other in a common defence, lies any hope of security.

As far as the British Army is concerned the 'post war' period of the last few decades has been marked, not only by a very large number of 'small wars' and warlike situations which, however unfortunate their origins have been, have made clear the necessity for military fitness and skill; it has also been marked by the maintenance, under solemn treaty, of a Field Force, at present the British Army of the Rhine, mechanised, trained and equipped to a high standard as part of the ultimate deterrent against major war itself, and as Britain's main contribution to the peace of Europe and the defence of our country and the countries of our NATO Allies.

Company Sergeant Major Gudgin of the 2nd Battalion in the trenches, 1917. The arm badges are just visible in this original snapshot.

Grenadier Battalions have served frequently in the British Army of the Rhine, latterly as mechanised battalions, part of armoured formations, trained to act in a mobile battle in close co-operation with armour. From there the modern Grenadier will suddenly find himself transposed either to deal with some emergency, to train far afield in distant lands with which training arrangements have been made, or to serve in the historic role of guarding the Sovereign and taking a principal part in the great ceremonial occasions of State which surround the British Crown. The modern Grenadier has to be as much at home in a 'flak jacket' and helmet on the streets in some 'internal security' situation, as in combat dress in the Armoured Personnel Carrier of an Armoured Division, or in scarlet tunic and distinctive bearskin cap on the Horse Guards Parade. In all these situations he shows the same qualities of adaptability, patience, humour, discipline and toughness which have enabled The Regiment to gain the name he bears.

* * *

Much of this short history has been concerned with fighting. Let us finish on a more celebratory note. In 1956, the Grenadiers enjoyed a Birthday, a very special Birthday. It was the Tercentenary or 300th anniversary of their formation by Charles II at Bruges in Flanders. Two battalions, the 2nd and the 3rd, were stationed in the London District, but the 1st Battalion, stationed in Germany, visited Bruges itself for a succession of ceremonies in the very beautiful city of its birth. Then the 1st Battalion travelled to England for a review of all three battalions; over 1,400 comrades attended – Grenadiers of all ages who had served in the

Regiment in the past. They came from all over the United Kingdom, an immense gathering, bringing together the youngest drummer with more than one who had served at the Battle of Omdurman in 1898. They came to Windsor Castle and there, in a parade which none who witnessed it will ever forget, were inspected by Her Majesty the Queen.

The Tercentenary was celebrated in various parts of the country where Grenadiers abound. In London the 3rd Battalion Trooped their Colour on the Queen's Birthday Parade. In St James's Palace a great exhibition of the trophies, pictures and treasures of the Regiment was displayed. In the Festival Hall a pageant and concert was presented to mark the occasion, followed by a huge banquet for 1,400 all ranks, serving and retired, past and present, young and old. More than once were recalled as appropriate the words of the Prince Consort, spoken on the occasion of the 200th anniversary a century before:

'That same discipline which has made this Regiment ever ready and terrible in war has enabled it to pass long periods of peace in the midst of all the temptations of a luxurious metropolis without loss of vigour and energy; to live in harmony and good fellowship with its fellow citizens; and to point to the remarkable fact that the Household Troops have now for two hundred years formed the permanent garrison of London; have always been at the command of the civil power to support law and order, but have never themselves disturbed that order, or given cause of complaint, either by insolence or licentiousness. Let us hope that for centuries to come these noble qualities may still shine forth, and that the Almighty will continue to shield and favour this little band of devoted soldiers.'

Escort and Colours, Chelsea Barracks, 1921.

The Plates

Uniform research by R. J. Marrion and D. S. V. Fosten

A1 Captain of Musketeers, 1685
A2 Captain of Grenadier Company, 1685
A3 Musketeer, 1685
A4 Grenadier, 1685

In 1685 the Regiment paraded for the Coronation of King James II. The Herald, James Sandford, has left a comprehensive record of the uniform of the Regiment on that day and this has been used as the

All orders of dress displayed here by members of the 3rd Battalion, 1923.

basis of this plate. The officers were not uniformly dressed at this time. Sandford states that although the majority wore scarlet coats faced with blue and laced with silver, others wore coats of rich crimson velvet. The Commanding Officer on that day was Lieutenant Colonel John Strode and he wore a coat of cloth of gold.

Grenadier companies had been added to infantry regiments some seven years earlier and their uniform was already being adapted for their particular service. The high-fronted caps were distinctive and are thought to have been designed to enable the soldiers to throw their bombs and to allow them to slip their fusil slings over their heads when in action, without snagging the broad-brimmed hats. The musketeers did not have fusil slings at this time.

The grenadier officer wears a plug bayonet and carries a powder flask. Although the portrait from which this figure is derived shows no fusil the equipment indicates that, even at this early period in the development of the grenadiers, their officers carried the same weapon as the men.

The Captain on the left wears, as a distinction of his rank, a large silver, gilded gorget, the last vestige of the half-armour worn during the Civil War. All dismounted officers carried the half-pike and on ceremonial occasions such as the Coronation it is likely that Lieutenant Colonel Strode would have marched at the head of his men armed with the same weapon.

The Regiment retained a company of Pikemen at this period. Although armed with 16 ft ash pikes they had discarded the pot helmets, corslets and tassets which had long been part of their uniform. They were now only distinguished by white worsted sashes with blue fringeing.

The Sergeants' rank distinctions are not recorded but what little evidence remains suggests that they would have worn the uniform of the soldiers with silver lace on the cuffs and over the seams.

Sandford records that the musketeers were armed with new snaphance muskets but still retained the old style 'bandolier of charges'. Sergeants were armed with halberds and officers carried swords, purchased privately and of non-uniform patterns.

B1 Private, Grenadier Company, 1704
B2 Officer, Battalion Company, 1704
B3 Private, Battalion Company, 1704

This plate illustrates the Regiment crossing the marshy meadows bordering the River Nebel at the Battle of Blenheim on 13 August 1704, when the regiment formed part of the leading brigade of Lord Cutts' attack on the village, which opened the battle. Clearing the treacherous swamp land, the Regiment came under murderous fire from the

French pallisades and the men fell in heaps; the remainder closed up unflinchingly, advancing until at least one third of the leading brigade had fallen including Brigadier Rowe and the two senior officers who tried to save him. The uniform is taken from Laguerre's paintings on the staircase walls at Marlborough House, London, and a print of the Regiment crossing the Nebel in the possession of the Regiment.

The long red coats had wide loose skirts without turnbacks at this period and the buttons and the decorative lace were placed right down the fronts. The wide cuffs and the small folded-down collar are distinctive features of the uniform, clearly shown in both sources. The lace on the coats of the rank and file was yellow at this period and not white; this is confirmed by the Laguerre painting, a print in the regimental archives and a newspaper account of the Coldstream.

Officers' coats were still not uniform in pattern although they were all in scarlet. The gold lace was laid on the coats in a variety of ways, but most figures in the Blenheim Tapestries show the style illustrated here. Although the Tapestries show officers wearing buttoned gaiters, even when mounted, Laguerre shows the soldiers with long white hose pulled over the knees.

The pattern headdress for the Grenadiers had now assumed the well-known mitre shape; many such headdresses in the decorative margins of the Tapestries indicate that the red crown at the back was often loose and hung backwards with pendent tassel, free from the stiff fronts. Sergeants now carried halberds, wore sashes, and had gold lace on the cuffs and seams of the coat.

C1 Drummer, 1792
C2 Sergeant, Grenadier Company, 1792
C3 Officer, Battalion Company, 1792
C4 Private, Battalion Company, 1792

In 1770 the King approved major alterations to the uniforms of the Regiment. These included the substitution of white linings for blue, the introduction of neat round cuffs instead of the old fashioned slash-and-frame pattern, and the introduction of plain white diamond-shaped looping. Flat pewter buttons replaced the old half-ball type and Sergeants replaced their old scarlet waistcoats with simpler and plainer white ones. Drummers' coats were also altered and the orange stripes in

Escort and Colours, Egypt, 1930; this was an interesting transitional period in uniform design.

their lace were discarded in favour of white silk and tinsel with interwoven blue fleurs-de-lys. Grenadiers were ordered to wear blue wings in lieu of the old red pattern, and corporals were now to wear white silk epaulettes in place of the old white worsted knots.

In 1786 the officers laid aside their espontoons and were now armed only with light swords. Grenadier Sergeants carried a light pattern fusil. In 1790 the Commander-in-Chief ordered that the regimental hats of the NCOs and men of the Brigade of Guards were, in future, to be worn without lace. The heavy and unwieldy halberds of the Sergeants were not discarded until 1792–93 and were then replaced with 9 ft pikes with cross bars.

The regimental grenadier cap was black bearskin with a lacquered front plate with white metal ornaments. The ornaments were gilded for the Officers and Sergeants. A print in the Regiment's possession shows a Light Infantry Sergeant in 1792. He wears a distinctive black 'round hat' with a curled brim and a black bearskin crest running from front to back over the crown. On the left side is a green feather. His coat is short-skirted and has blue facings and gold lace. The wings are blue laced gold with gold shoulder-knots over them, and he has a square-cut white waistcoat and long white fitted gaiter-trousers which shaped over the shoes. He is armed with a light fusil. Officers of this company wore a similar black cap but with a round-topped crown covered with the bearskin crest. They wore short-skirted jackets and carried sharply curved sabres in black leather scabbards with gilt mounts from long slings, and wore tight white web pantaloons and short boots. A Regimental Order of 1797 stated that Officers of the Light Infantry Company were always to mount Guard in their jackets unless in Full Dress.

D1 Adjutant, 1815
D2 Sergeant, Light Company, 1815
D3 Private, Grenadier Company, 1815
D4 Drummer, 1815

The plate illustrates the Regiment at Waterloo, 18 June 1815. The seated officer is the Adjutant. The General Order of 1809, which prescribed that Captains of the Foot Guards should in future wear two epaulettes as a mark of their rank also directed that the Adjutant was to wear one epaulette on the

Two Guardsmen about 1941/42. Note the white flash painted on the left side of the steel helmet; 1937 webbing is worn with the gas mask on the chest and the gas cape rolled on the shoulders. The furthest soldier is armed with the old No. 1 Mk III Lee Enfield with its 17 in sword bayonet; the other has the newly introduced No. 4 Mk I with its spike bayonet.

Major-General A. H. S. Adair, DSO, MC, commanding general of the Guards Armoured Division, entering Brussels on 4 September 1944 in a Cromwell tank. The divisional insignia is just visible on the off side of the front hull plate. (Studio L'essor)

The capture of Nijmegen Bridge by the 1st and 2nd Battalions.

right shoulder but with the addition of a laced regimental strap on the left. The Quartermaster was ordered to wear one epaulette on the right shoulder, and Sergeant Majors to wear two regimental laced straps (as worn by the Adjutant on his left shoulder).

When the high-fronted shako was introduced in 1811–12 the Prince Regent was pleased to allow the regiments of Foot Guards to add gold-laced rims around the high fronts of the officers' caps and brass rims around the fronts of the caps of the soldiers. This proved unsatisfactory for some reason, and shortly afterwards the decorations were discontinued. However, French drawings of the Foot Guards in Paris after the campaign show Drum Majors and Bandsmen still wearing some form of fancy yellow metal edging to these caps. A regimental order of 1812 ordered that black tape strings be fitted to the sides of the caps of the 1st Battalion when on active service; these were to tie under the soldiers' chins. The central figure is a grenadier and has a white shako tuft. The centre companies wore white over red tufts in their caps and the light infantry company had green tufts and, in addition, had a small brass bugle-horn fixed above their shako plates. In full dress the grenadier company still wore black bearskin caps. However, these expensive headdresses were not taken on campaign and were taken into store until the battalions returned home. The shako covers are clearly shown in Dighton's several water colours and larger battle paintings of Waterloo. They are also indicated in the sketches by Captain Jones and in the Hamilton-Smith plates, although the latter have a somewhat different design.

The colour of the pantaloons at this period seems not to have been uniform. There are references in regimental orders to grey pantaloons but also to white Russian duck, and Dighton chose to show the Coldstream fighting outside Hougoumont in these white trousers worn over white gaiters. Hamilton-Smith, on the other hand, shows the 1st Foot Guards, either in grey trousers worn over black gaiters, or in what seem to be lighter and closer fitting grey pantaloons tucked into gaiters. In 1810 a Regimental Order permitted the officers of the Regiment to wear blue pantaloons or overalls when on the march, although in full dress white buckskins or tight fitting web pantaloons with hessians or hussar boots were worn.

E1 Officer, 1854
E2 Guardsman, 1854
E3 Drummer, 1854
E4 Colour Sergeant, 1854

On 5 November 1854 the Regiment fought the

Battle of Inkerman in greatcoats. A painting, alleged to have been based on information given to the artist by soldiers of the Regiment who fought in the action, shows NCOs and men dressed in caped greatcoats and bearskin caps. Most men were equipped with two shoulder-belts supporting the cartridge pouch and the bayonet. Some had canvas haversacks and wooden water canteens. The overcoats of the NCOs had blue collars and cuffs by regulation. Photographs reveal officers invariably wearing the blue braided frock and service caps. The 1846 Regulations prescribed a dark-blue cap with a black braided band, gilt grenade badge and a drooping peak edged with gold lace. It was worn with a waterproof cover. However, most officers seem to have preferred the adaptable Albert cap, as shown here.

A dark-blue cloak lined with scarlet shalloon was the regulation top garment but service conditions prompted the use of dark-grey caped overcoats similar to those worn by the men. Lady Butler's 'Roll Call' and Robert Gibbs's 'The Guards at Inkerman' show officers wearing this caped coat and the bearskin cap.

The Adjutant wore the uniform of his rank, while the Quartermaster wore a scarlet coatee with blue collar and cuffs and with silver embroidered grenades only on his collar fronts. He wore Subalterns' epaulettes and a silk-bound cocked hat with a gold loop, crimson and gold tassels and a white feather. The Solicitor wore a plain blue coatee with red collar and cuffs and regimental buttons and a plain cocked hat with a black loop and button and no plume. The Quartermaster had the sash and appointments of other officers; the Solicitor wore no sword.

The mens' equipment was not pipe-clayed in the Crimea, neither was the black leather of the pouches and bayonet sheaths blackballed. Consequently the belts and straps reverted to a darkish buff and the other leather became scuffed and cracked. The coatees and overcoats were seriously affected by the weather. The dye of the coatees faded to a purplish brown, the blue facings faded and the overcoats became more brown than grey. Bearskins were reduced to a height of 9 in. Officers carried the 1822-pattern sword with gilt, half-basket guard with the Royal Cypher insert. It had a black leather scabbard with gilt mounts and a

Company Sergeant Major, Regimental Sergeant Major and Drum Major, Tripoli, 1948.

crimson and gold knot with bullion tassel. The Field Officers and the Adjutant had brass scabbards. Sergeants carried special regimental pattern swords with brass hilts with grenade badges set in the knuckle bow guard, and buff leather knots. Their scabbards were black with brass mounts. Officers carried 1848-pattern Colts or 1851-type Adams revolvers.

The rank and file were armed with the Minié rifle. It was 6 ft and $\frac{1}{2}$ in long when the 17 in bayonet was fixed, and weighed about 10 lbs. The weapon had a calibre of .702 in and a range of about 250 yds, although good results were possible over much longer distances.

Members of the 3rd Battalion in Malaya, 1949.

Inspection of HQ UNFICYP Guard; the Queen's Company, 1st Battalion, with the United Nations Force, Cyprus, in 1965.

Men of No. 2 Company, 1st Battalion emplaning for Bahrein from RAF Sharjah, 1969.

F1 Guardsman, Egypt, 1882
F2 Guardsman, Omdurman, 1898
F3 Guardsman, Camel Regt, Gordon Relief Expedition, 1884–85

The latter half of the 19th century saw a proliferation of 'small wars' throughout the British Empire, culminating in the Boer War of 1899. During this period experiments were made to produce a comfortable service dress. During the Egyptian Campaign of 1882, British troops from the United Kingdom wore unlined scarlet frocks, the only concession to the sun being a white helmet, which was officially introduced for foreign service during the Abyssinian Campaign of 1868. The frock had a blue collar with a white worsted grenade each side. A Regimental Order dated 22 July 1881 stated that officers were to provide themselves with a scarlet frock similar to the men with white grenades on the collar and gold badges of rank worn on the scarlet shoulder straps. A further order recommended officers proceeding to the Mediterranean to take two red (sic) serge frocks on active service. The Guards stained their helmets on the voyage out from England. Officers wore regimental badges in the paggri at the front of the helmet.

The Gordon Relief Expedition, 1884–85, saw soldiers of the Desert Column issued with an experimental grey serge jacket with cord breeches and blue puttees. Members of the Camel Regiments were also issued with blue woollen fisherman style jumpers for wear at night. To enable regiments to be readily identifiable, numerals and letters were cut from old scarlet serge frocks and stitched to the right upper sleeve. The white buff waist-belt was withdrawn by a Regimental Order dated 23 September 1884, and was replaced by a brown leather belt with a snake clasp.

Thirteen years later, a British army moved on Omdurman to end the Dervish rule, and all were clothed in lightweight drab clothing. At the onset of the Boer War the lightweight clothing had become established, but the arduous conditions encountered in South Africa soon reduced these to rags. Helmets were an encumbrance and the buff leather Slade Wallace equipment was found wanting. Towards the end of the war a heavier drab clothing was issued, the Slade Wallace pouches were replaced by a cotton web bandolier and helmets by a felt slouch hat favoured by the Dominion forces. During the Boer War the Grenadier Guards wore a small white hair plume in the left side of both helmet and slouch hat, but during the 1898 Sudan Campaign a crimson and blue 'flash' or cockade resembling a grenade was worn on both sides of the helmet.

G1 Lieutenant, 1914–15
G2 Guardsman, North Africa, 1942–43
G3 Guardsman, Guards Armoured Division, NW Europe, 1944–45

An Army Order dated 17 January 1902 sanctioned the first khaki field service dress for officers and other ranks. It was described as 'drab serge clothing'; the other ranks pattern remained virtually unchanged until 1937. Officers uniforms underwent a number of minor changes, mainly in the method of displaying rank; at first this was shown by a system of drab braids placed vertically above the cuff, each braid terminating with a 'crows foot'. In November 1902 this was superseded by a system of braid rings on each cuff with a flap superimposed on these on which the normal stars and crowns were displayed. This, in turn (as a war time innovation), was replaced by the rank insignia, worn on shoulder straps, which became official in 1922. Officers of the Guards have always worn a distinctive shade of khaki which can be best described as khaki minus the hint of green.

A new service dress was introduced in 1937. Called 'battle dress', this gradually began to replace the old 1902 pattern, although the changeover was not completed until late 1940. At the same time a new webbing equipment replaced the '08 pattern web equipment and was worn by the entire British Army from 1940. Our Guardsman in North Africa is wearing khaki drill shorts (irreverently termed 'Bombay Bloomers' by the rank and file) and shirt with the web equipment reduced to light marching order. His helmet displays a symbolic white 'plume' on the left side. The temperature fell drastically at night in the desert and when possible pullovers, battledress blouse, or greatcoats were worn over the 'KD' uniform. To supplement his normal ·303 No. 1 Mk III Lee Enfield rifle, our Grenadier also carries a captured Italian Beretta M 3A sub-machine gun.

The last winter of World War Two saw the introduction of a heavy canvas one-piece tank suit which had a detachable hood and which could also be utilized as a sleeping bag. Known as the 'pixie suit', this lasted as a garment for armoured crews until well into the 1960s. Prior to this, black overalls worn over the standard battledress very early in the war soon gave way to denim overalls, or alternatively the battledress with a sleeveless leather jerkin worn over the top. Personal armament was a pistol carried in a '37 pattern web holster and waist-belt. Although withdrawn in 1943–44, a thigh holster, originally issued to armoured personnel, was still much favoured and, according to veterans, retained quite unofficially by drivers.

The Senior Major and Quartermasters, 1st Battalion at Caterham Barracks, 1968: Lieutenant (QM) J. R. Dann, Major E. H. L. Aubrey-Fletcher, Captain (QM) F. J. Clutton.

H1 Captain, Frockcoat Order, 1970s
H2 Regimental Sergeant Major, Full Dress, 1970s
H3 Guardsman, Internal Security kit, 1970s

The officer is dressed in Frockcoat; the following regimental officers only are allowed to wear this order of dress:

The Colonel of the Regiment
The Lieutenant Colonel Commanding the Regiment
Commanding Officers of Battalions
Seconds in Command (Senior Majors) of Battalions

Men of the anti-tank company, 1st Battalion, serving a Mobat recoilless anti-tank gun in the Persian Gulf, 1969. (HQ London District PRO)

The Regimental Adjutant, Adjutants and Assistant Adjutants
The Director of Music
Regimental Officers in certain appointments at the Guards Depot and on the Staff at HQ London District and HQ Household Division.

The braided form of frockcoat was first worn about 1831 and has remained virtually unchanged to the present day. It is worn with overalls and blue forage cap; the Director of Music wears trousers in place of overalls. Medals are never worn with this order of dress, only ribbons.

The Sergeant Major is depicted wearing Full Dress. Only the following Warrant Officers Class I are entitled to wear the large Coat of Arms in all orders of dress: The Superintending Clerk at Regimental Headquarters, at HQ Household Division and at the Guards Depot.
Regimental Sergeant Majors of Battalions (known as 'The Sergeant Major')
Regimental Sergeant Majors of the Guards Depot
Extra-regimentally employed WO1s who have held one of the above appointments
The Garrison Sergeant Major, London District

In Full Dress, remaining Sergeant Majors wear a small Coat of Arms at the bottom of the sleeve; Regimental Quartermaster Sergeant and Orderly Room Quartermaster Sergeant wear a crown surrounded by a laurel wreath at the bottom of the sleeve. In No. 1 Dress – now worn only unofficially – and No. 2 Dress all the above ranks and the Drill Sergeant are entitled to wear a Sam Browne belt. Drill Sergeants and Company Sergeant Majors are Warrant Officers Class II, and in Full Dress wear a colour badge on the right upper sleeve. The carrying of the pace stick when on duty and on parade is the entitlement of the following Warrant Officers and NCOs:
Garrison and Regimental Sergeant Majors
Warrant and Non-Commissioned Officer drill instructors at the Royal Military Academy, Sandhurst
Drill Sergeants
Company Sergeant Majors serving at the Guards Depot and Army Department Schools as Instructors
Superintendent Sergeants at the Guards Depot

The red sash is worn by all Warrant Officers, Colour Sergeants and Sergeants on parade or duty in uniform. That of Warrant Officers is in silk, and that of Colour Sergeants and Sergeants is in worsted. White gloves are worn in Full Dress by all Warrant Officers and NCOs from the rank of Sergeant upwards. Swords are worn by all Warrant Officers and by the following NCOs in Full Dress:
Warrant Officers Class I
Regimental Quartermaster Sergeants
Drill Sergeants
Orderly Room Sergeants (whether WOs or NCOs)
Drum Majors
Master Tailors
The Band Sergeant Major

Warrant Officer Class I and the Regimental Quartermaster Sergeant wear a gold sword knot in Full Dress, and the remainder a knot in white buff leather.

The final figure is dressed in Internal Security kit. He wears the camouflaged or 'disruptive pattern' combat clothing, with fragmentation vest – 'flak jacket' – over the top. His webbing is reduced and can be adapted to meet the needs of any situation, and the rifle sling is attached to the wrist instead of to the butt swivel to prevent the weapon being snatched away. The brass regimental grenade badge on the khaki beret is blackened. Short khaki puttees are worn about the ankles. During one tour in Northern Ireland, boots were adapted regimentally to resemble the American style of combat boot by having an extra piece of leather attached at the ankle; this saved the moments required to wind and tie the puttee when the troops were called out at short notice.

Her Majesty The Queen

when Her Royal Highness The Princess Elizabeth, 24 February 1942

THE COLONELS OF THE REGIMENT

1 **Thomas, Lord Wentworth 26 Aug 1660**
2 **John Russell 23 Nov 1661**
3 **Henry, Duke of Grafton,** KG **14 Dec 1680**
4 **Edward, Earl of Lichfield 13 Nov 1688**
5 **Henry, Earl of Romney 16 Mar 1689**
6 **Charles, Duke of Schomberg 27 Dec 1691**
7 **John, Duke of Marlborough,** KG **23 Apr 1704**
8 **James, Duke of Ormond,** KG **1 Jan 1712**
9 **William, Earl of Cadogan,** KP **18 June 1722**
10 **Sir Charles Wills,** KB **6 Aug 1726**
11 **Field Marshal H.R.H. William, Duke of Cumberland,** KG **18 Feb 1742**
12 **Field Marshal John, Earl Ligonier,** KB **30 Nov 1757**
13 **Field Marshal H.R.H. William, Duke of Gloucester,** KG **30 Apr 1770**
14 **Field Marshal H.R.H. Frederick, Duke of York,** KG, GCB, GCH **5 Sept 1805**
15 **Field Marshal Arthur, Duke of Wellington,** KG, GCB, GCH **22 Jan 1827**
16 **Field Marshal H.R.H. Albert, Prince of Saxe Coburg and Gotha,** KG, KT, KP, GCMG **28 Sept 1852**
17 **Field Marshal H.R.H. George, Duke of Cambridge,** KG, KP, GCB, GCMG, GCH **15 Dec 1861**
18 **Field Marshal H.R.H. Arthur, Duke of Connaught and Strathearn,** KG, KT, KP, GCB, GCSI, GCMG, GCIE, GCVO, GBE, VD, TD **1 May 1904**
19 **H.R.H. The Princess Elizabeth 24 Apr 1942**
20 **General the Lord Jeffreys,** KCB, KCVO, CMG, DL **8 Apr 1952**
21 **Major General Sir Allan Adair, Bt,** KCVO, CB, DSO, MC, DL, JP **19 Dec 1960**
22 **Field Marshal H.R.H. The Prince Philip Duke of Edinburgh** KG, KT, OM, GBE **1975**

Helicopter training at Chelsea Barracks, 1975. (HQ London District PRO)

THE COLOURS AND THE REGIMENTAL BADGE AND MOTTO

Each Battalion has two Colours, The Queen's Colour and The Regimental Colour. In the Foot Guards, unlike regiments of the line, The Queen's Colour is crimson and the Regimental Colour is the Great Union. In addition the regiment has the Queen's Company Colour, the correct designation of which is 'The Queen's Company Colour, The Royal Standard of The Regiment'.

Forty-four of the seventy-six Battle Honours appear on the Queen's and Regimental Colours.

In addition, there are thirty Camp Colours which are allocated to Battalions and Companies of the Regiment.

All battalions of the Regiment have the right to march through the City of London with colours flying, drums beating and bayonets fixed.

The badge of the Regiment is the Royal Cypher reversed and interlaced, surrounded by the Garter and surmounted by the Tudor Crown.

The Grenade is a secondary badge.

The Regimental motto is 'HONI SOIT QUI MAL Y PENSE', meaning 'EVIL BE TO HIM WHO EVIL THINKS'.

THE QUEEN'S COMPANY

The Queen's Company has the privilege of being on duty in Westminster Abbey on the occasion of the Coronation of the Sovereign.

The Queen's Company performs the duty of watching over the dead body of the Sovereign prior to any public lying-in-State. The Company also provides the bearer party at the Sovereign's funeral.

The officer appointed by the Sovereign to command the Queen's Company is always referred to as 'The Captain of The Queen's Company', irrespective of the rank he may hold.

The Queens' Company Colour is only carried when The Queen is present.

REGIMENTAL MUSIC

Regimental Marches

Slow Marches
- The March from 'Scipio'
- The Duke of York's March

Quick Marches
- The British Grenadier
- The Grenadiers' March (also sometimes used as a slow march)

The March from 'Scipio' was composed for the First Guards by Handel, and was presented to the Regiment before its inclusion in the opera, which was first performed in 1726. The 'Duke of York's March' was adopted as a Slow March by the Regiment during the Colonelcy of the Duke of York in 1805. The two quick marches were the marching tunes of the Grenadier Companies of the whole Army. They were adopted by the First Guards on becoming a Regiment of Grenadiers in 1815; the Regiment marches past in quick time to 'The British Grenadiers', and into camp or Barracks to 'The Grenadiers' March'.

The Regimental band is composed of musicians under a Director of Music; the bass drummer is known as the 'Time Beater'. Each battalion has its own Corps of Drums (fifes and drums) under a Drum Major.